everyday Writing
Intervention Activities

D1209435

Table of Contents

Using Everyday Writing Intervention Activities ii

Unit 1: Choose an Idea 1

Unit 2: Narrow the Writing Idea 7

Unit 3: Develop the Writing Idea. 13

Unit 4: Develop an Outline of Information 19

Unit 5: Strong Nonfiction Leads 25

Unit 6: Strong Fiction Leads 31

Unit 7: Develop a Plot 37

Unit 8: Develop a Character 43

Unit 9: Strong Nonfiction Endings 49

Unit 10: Strong Fiction Endings. 55

Unit 11: What Is Voice?. 61

Unit 12: Using Different Voices. 67

Unit 13: Adjectives. 73

Unit 14: Adverbs. 79

Unit 15: Strong Verbs. 85

Unit 16: Nouns. 91

Unit 17: Idioms 97

Unit 18: Similes. 103

Unit 19: What Is a Sentence? 109

Unit 20: Varying Sentence Structure 115

Using Everyday Writing Intervention Activities

Research shows that reading and writing are reciprocal processes, and often the same students who struggle as readers need support to develop their writing skills.

The Everyday Writing Intervention Activities provides developmentally appropriate, easy-to-use, five-day writing units for Grades K–5. Each unit focuses on a particular writing process or writer's craft skill and provides multiple opportunities for students to practice that skill. As students complete these engaging mini-lessons, they will build a repertoire of writing skills they can apply as they write independently during writer's workshops, respond to texts they have read, complete content-area writing assignments, or write to prompts on standardized assessments.

These units are structured around a research-based model-guide-practice-apply approach. You can use these activities in a variety of intervention models, including Response to Intervention (RTI).

Getting Started

In just five simple steps, Everyday Writing Intervention Activities provides everything you need to identify students' needs and to provide targeted intervention.

online

1. PRE-ASSESS to identify students'
writing needs. Use the pre-assessment to identify the skills your students need to master.

Day 1

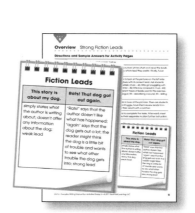

2. MODEL the skill.
Every five-day unit targets a specific writing study area. On Day 1, use the teacher prompts and reproducible activity page to introduce and model the skill.

Day 2   **Day 3**   **Day 4**

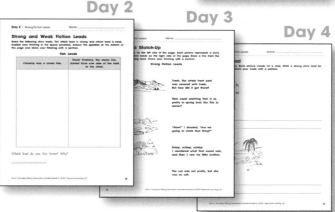

3. GUIDE, PRACTICE, and APPLY.
Use the reproducible practice activities for Days 2, 3, and 4 to build students' understanding and skill proficiency.

Day 5

4. MONITOR progress.
Administer the Day 5 reproducible assessment to monitor each student's progress and to make instructional decisions.

5. POST-ASSESS to document student progress.
Use the post-assessment to measure students' progress as a result of your interventions.

online

Standards-Based Writing Awareness & Writing Skills in Everyday Intervention Activities

The writing strategies found in the Everyday Intervention Activities series are introduced developmentally and spiral from one grade to the next. The chart below shows the types of words and skill areas addressed at each grade level in this series.

Everyday Writing Intervention Activities Series Skills	K	1	2	3	4	5
Choosing a topic	✔	✔	✔	✔	✔	✔
Narrow the focus	✔	✔	✔	✔	✔	✔
Develop the idea (list what I know, research, complete list)	✔	✔	✔	✔	✔	✔
Organizing ideas/Writing an outline	✔	✔	✔	✔	✔	✔
Strong leads (fiction)	✔	✔	✔	✔	✔	✔
Strong leads (nonfiction)	✔	✔	✔	✔	✔	✔
Developing a character	✔	✔	✔	✔	✔	✔
Developing a plot	✔	✔	✔	✔	✔	✔
Strong endings (fiction)	✔	✔	✔	✔	✔	✔
Strong endings (nonfiction)	✔	✔	✔	✔	✔	✔
What is voice?	✔	✔	✔	✔	✔	✔
How do I write in my voice?	✔	✔	✔	✔	✔	✔
Different voices	✔	✔	✔	✔	✔	✔
Adjectives	✔	✔	✔	✔	✔	✔
Adverbs	✔	✔	✔	✔	✔	✔
Verbs	✔	✔	✔	✔	✔	✔
Nouns	✔	✔	✔	✔		
Advanced nouns					✔	✔
Idioms			✔	✔	✔	✔
Similes			✔	✔	✔	✔
Metaphors					✔	✔
Personification						✔

Using Everyday Intervention for RTI

According to the National Center on Response to Intervention, RTI "integrates assessment and intervention within a multi-level prevention system to maximize student achievement and to reduce behavior problems." This model of instruction and assessment allows schools to identify at-risk students, monitor their progress, provide research-proven interventions, and "adjust the intensity and nature of those interventions depending on a student's responsiveness."

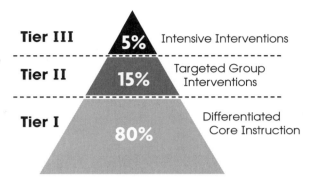

RTI models vary from district to district, but the most prevalent model is a three-tiered approach to instruction and assessment.

The Three Tiers of RTI	Using Everyday Intervention Activities
Tier I: Differentiated Core Instruction • Designed for all students • Preventive, proactive, standards-aligned instruction • Whole- and small-group differentiated instruction • Daily literacy instruction	• Use whole-group writing mini-lessons to introduce and guide practice with vocabulary strategies that all students need to learn. • Use any or all of the units in the order that supports your core instructional program.
Tier II: Targeted Group Interventions • For struggling readers and writers • Provide thirty minutes of daily instruction beyond the Tier I core literacy instruction • Instruction is conducted in small groups of three to five students with similar needs	• Select units based on your students' areas of need (the pre-assessment can help you identify these). • Use the units as week-long, small-group mini-lessons.
Tier III: Intensive Interventions • For high-risk students experiencing considerable difficulty in reading and writing • Provide up to sixty minutes of additional intensive intervention each day in addition to the ninety-minute Tier I core reading instruction • More intense and explicit instruction • Instruction conducted individually or with smaller groups of one to three students with similar needs	• Select units based on your students' areas of need. • Use the units as one component of an intensive reading and writing intervention program.

Overview Choose an Idea

Directions and Sample Answers for Activity Pages

Day 1	See "Provide a Real-World Example" below.
Day 2	Read the title and directions aloud. Give each student a paper bag. Ask students to think about the word **idea**. Have them answer the questions and share responses with a partner. Then ask students to decorate their idea bag using illustrations that explain their **idea** thoughts. Ask students to keep their Idea Bags in their desks.
Day 3	Read the title and directions aloud. Place students in pairs and give each student three note cards. Ask students to look at the picture and identify everything about the scene, including people, animals, objects, location, and actions. Finally, have students choose three ideas about the picture that interest them most, write them on note cards (one idea per note card) and place the cards in their Idea Bags. Remind students that they can use these ideas any time they need a writing idea.
Day 4	Read the title and directions aloud. Place students in pairs and give each student three note cards. Have pairs think about and write three ideas that interest them. Then have pairs share what interests them about each idea. Finally, have students write their ideas on note cards (one idea per card), and place them in their Idea Bags. Tell students not to worry about knowing enough about or writing about the ideas.
Day 5	Read the directions aloud. Invite students to choose three ideas that interest them. (If students struggle, provide examples for them.) Then ask students to complete the chart and answer the questions at the bottom of the page. Discuss their results. Use their responses to plan further instruction.

Provide a Real-World Example

Ideas Chart

Idea	I like this idea.	I know about this idea.	I want to learn more.
seashells	Yes	No	No
mountains	Yes	Yes	Yes
New York City	Yes	Yes	No
music	Yes	Yes	No
dogs	Yes	Yes	Yes

◆ Hand out the Day 1 activity page. **Say:** *One of the hardest things writers do is choose an idea to write about. The three important things to remember are: choose an idea that interests you, choose an idea that you know something about, and choose an idea you want to learn more about because you will probably research your idea. This applies to fiction and nonfiction.*

◆ Write the three important things on chart paper and leave them hanging in the room. Show a copy of the Day 1 handout on the overhead or copy it onto the board.

◆ **Say:** *Look at the chart. I wrote five things that interest me, but I don't really want to write about all of them. Watch as I choose a writing idea that works for me. I like seashells, but I really don't know much about them, and I'm not interested in learning more right now.* Place a **Yes** or **No** in the appropriate columns. **Say:** *I love mountains and know quite a bit about them. I'm very interested in how they form.* (Use the completed chart to continue the process.)

◆ **Say:** *It looks like I am most interested in writing about mountains and dogs. Now I just need to decide between the two. Mountains are cool. I could write about different mountain ranges. I'd need to do some research. Dogs are cool, too. There are so many different kinds of dogs, and I could always write about how to take care of them. I think I like dogs better than mountains. Remember, all writers choose ideas, and choosing ideas is not always easy. Take your time and think about what you like and don't like before you make a decision.*

Choose an Idea

Listen to your teacher. Then complete the chart.

Ideas Chart

Idea	I like this idea.	I know about this idea.	I want to learn more.
seashells			
mountains			
New York City			
music			
dogs			

My Idea Bag

Complete the activity with a partner.

"Hmm. What do I think about that?"

Think about the word **idea**. Write your thoughts in the space and share your thinking with a partner.

_____

_____

What is an idea?

_____

What do you think about when you hear the word **idea**?

_____

Write "Idea Bag" on the paper bag. Decorate your bag with pictures that explain your **idea** thoughts.

Picture This

Look at the picture. Write down everything you see in the picture, including the people and things around them, what they are doing, and where they are.

_____ _____ _____

_____ _____ _____

_____ _____ _____

_____ _____ _____

_____ _____ _____

Read your ideas. Choose three ideas that interest you most. Share your choices with your partner. Write each idea on a note card and place the cards in your Idea Bag.

Writing Ideas

Think about what interests you.
Choose three things and write them on the lines.

_____

_____

_____

What interests you about each idea?

_____

_____

_____

Write one idea on each of the three note cards provided.
Place the note cards in your Idea Bag.

Assessment

Look at the following chart. In the left-hand column write three ideas that interest you. Then complete the chart using pluses and minuses.

Ideas Chart

Idea	I like this idea.	I know about this idea.	I want to learn more.

Use the chart to answer the questions.

Which ideas will you not choose? Why not?

Which ideas might you choose? Why?

Look at your answer for the previous question. Will you need to research those ideas before you can write?

Which writing idea do you choose?

Overview   Narrow the Writing Idea

Directions and Sample Answers for Activity Pages

Day 1	See "Provide a Real-World Example" below.
Day 2	Read the title and directions aloud. Invite students to read the list of games. Then ask them to organize the list into meaningful groups and give each group a title. Finally, ask students to think about which group they would like to write about. Ask them to share their thinking with a partner. Remind students that there are many ways to organize the list.
Day 3	Read the title and directions aloud. Invite students to look at the pictures. Then ask students to write a list of ten things they think of when they see each picture. Remind students that there are no wrong answers. Students will use their ideas in the next lesson.
Day 4	Read the title and directions aloud. Invite students to review their lists from the previous lesson. Ask students to choose one list and organize the list into groups. Give each group a title. Finally, ask students to think about which group they would like to write about and share their thinking with a partner.
Day 5	Read the directions aloud. Allow time for students to complete the first task. Next, have students complete the second task. Afterward, meet individually with students. Discuss their results. Use their responses to plan further instruction.

Provide a Real-World Example

◆ Hand out the Day 1 activity page.

◆ Write the word **dogs** on the board. **Say:** *I've decided to write about dogs. There are so many things about dogs that I like. How am I going to decide what idea to write about? Watch as I choose one thing to write about. First, I'll make a list of things that have to do with dogs.*

◆ Generate a list of **dog** ideas using the terms shown. **Say:** *Wow. That's a long list. And it's not organized. For me to make up my mind, I need to understand what I just wrote. I'm going to put these ideas into groups. I notice that I've listed types of dogs. I'll write those in a list.* Write the types of dogs in one list: boxer, dachshund, German shepherd.

◆ **Say:** *I've also listed what dogs need to stay clean. I'll write those in another list.* Write what dogs need to stay clean in another list. Then repeat for the other categories.

◆ **Say:** *Now I need to review each group and label them so I know what the groups are about.* Review each group and label them with the following titles: "Types of Dogs," "What Dogs Need to Stay Clean," and "What Dogs Need Around the House."

◆ **Say:** *Wow. I've just taken lots of ideas and organized them into categories. Now I need to decide what I'm going to write about. I don't want to write about types of dogs or what dogs need around the house. I think I really want to write about keeping a dog clean. Organizing my ideas really helped me make a good decision.*

Dogs	Types of Dogs	What Dogs Need to Stay Clean	What Dogs Need Around the House
brushes	boxer	brushes	toys
boxer	dachshund	baths	balls
baths	German shepherd	flea powder	
dachshund			
German shepherd			
flea powder			
toys			
balls			

Narrow the Writing Idea

Write a list of everything you think of when you hear the word *dogs*.

Dogs

1. _____

2. _____

3. _____

4. _____

5. _____

6. _____

7. _____

8. _____

9. _____

10. _____

Group the ideas into categories. Then give each group a title.

Title: _____   **Title:** _____   **Title:** _____

1. _____   1. _____   1. _____

2. _____   2. _____   2. _____

3. _____   3. _____   3. _____

4. _____   4. _____   4. _____

5. _____   5. _____   5. _____

Organize Ideas

Read the list of games.

football	soccer	puzzles
cards	chess	jacks
dominoes	baseball	basketball

Organize the list into groups. Then give each group a title.

Title: _____   **Title:** _____   **Title:** _____

1. _____   **1.** _____   **1.** _____

2. _____   **2.** _____   **2.** _____

3. _____   **3.** _____   **3.** _____

Think about each group. Which group would you like to write about most? Why? Share your thinking with a partner.

Writing Your Ideas

Look at the pictures. For each picture, write ten things that you think about when you see the picture.

1. _____
2. _____
3. _____
4. _____
5. _____

6. _____
7. _____
8. _____
9. _____
10. _____

1. _____
2. _____
3. _____
4. _____
5. _____

6. _____
7. _____
8. _____
9. _____
10. _____

Narrow the Focus

Look at your lists from Day 3. Choose one list and organize the list into groups. Give each group a label. Think about each group. Which group would you like to write about? Why? Share your thinking with a partner.

Title: _____

1. _____

2. _____

3. _____

4. _____

5. _____

Title: _____

1. _____

2. _____

3. _____

4. _____

5. _____

Title: _____

1. _____

2. _____

3. _____

4. _____

5. _____

Title: _____

1. _____

2. _____

3. _____

4. _____

5. _____

Assessment

Look at the picture. Under the picture, write ten things that you think about when you see the picture.

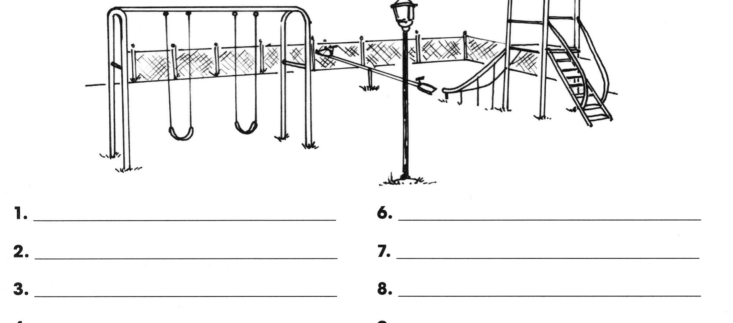

1. _____

2. _____

3. _____

4. _____

5. _____

6. _____

7. _____

8. _____

9. _____

10. _____

In the space below, organize the list into groups. Then give each group a title.

Title: _____

1. _____

2. _____

3. _____

4. _____

5. _____

Title: _____

1. _____

2. _____

3. _____

4. _____

5. _____

Title: _____

1. _____

2. _____

3. _____

4. _____

5. _____

Think about each group. Which group would you like to write about most? Why?

Overview   Develop the Writing Idea

Directions and Sample Answers for Activity Pages

Day 1	See "Provide a Real-World Example" below.
Day 2	Read the title and directions aloud. Ask students to identify two things that they already know about each idea. Ask students to write those ideas on the lines provided and share their ideas with a partner.
Day 3	Read the title and directions aloud. Tell students that each picture stands for a possible writing idea. Ask students to think about each idea and identify two questions for each idea that they would like answered. Have students write their questions on the lines provided. Finally, ask students to share their questions with a partner. Remind students that each question could be used later to develop a writing idea.
Day 4	Read the title and directions aloud. Invite students to read the list of ideas. Ask students to research each idea using encyclopedias or the Internet and identify two things that they did not know about each idea. Have students write the information on the lines provided and share their thoughts with a partner.
Day 5	Read the directions aloud. Allow time for students to complete the task. Afterward, meet individually with students. Discuss their results. Use their responses to plan further instruction.

Provide a Real-World Example

◆ Draw a knowledge chart on the board or overhead. Hand out the Day 1 activity page.

◆ Write the phrase **dog bath** on the board. **Say:** *I've decided to write about giving a dog a bath. I want to include certain things, so I need to plan, or develop, my idea before I write. Asking a question helps me plan.* Write the question on the board: *Why do dogs need baths?*

◆ **Say:** *Answers to this question will help me plan my idea. I'll use a knowledge chart to help me plan my idea.* Use the completed knowledge chart here to model how to develop a writing idea. **Say:** *I know dogs get really dirty from playing outside. The dirt sticks to their hair and then it drops on the floor in the house. I also know dogs get fleas on them. Those are nasty, and I don't want those in my house. Both of these ideas are reasons for a dog bath. I'll write those things into the chart. Is that all I want to include in my paper? What questions do I have about dog baths? Well, I don't know what kind of soap is best for a dog bath. Do I need to buy flea soap or just regular dog soap? Also, how often do they need a bath? I'll write those questions on the chart.*

Knowledge Chart

Question	What do I know?	Is this enough information?	What questions do I have?
Why do dogs need baths?	They get dirty outside and then track the dirt inside. They get fleas and then bring the fleas inside.	No	What kind of soap is best for a dog bath? How often does a dog need a bath?

◆ Circle the last column containing the questions. **Say:** *I don't have answers to the questions in the last column. I'll need to do a little research on the Internet before I can write my paper. I can probably find information in the encyclopedia, but I like the Internet better so I'll use that.*

◆ Remind students that developing a writing idea takes time and students should not rush this part of the writing process.

Develop the Writing Idea

Complete the chart below.

Knowledge Chart

Question	What do I know?	Is this enough information?	What questions do I have?
Why do dogs need baths?			

What Do You Know About It?

Read the list of ideas. For each idea, identify two things that you already know. Write your ideas on the lines and share your information with a partner.

dinosaurs

_____

_____

birthday parties

_____

_____

tennis shoes

_____

_____

playground slides

_____

_____

Ask a Question ... or Two

Look at the pictures. Each picture stands for a different writing idea. Think about two questions that you have for each idea. Write your questions on the lines and share them with a partner.

money

_____

_____

_____

sports car

_____

_____

_____

teachers

_____

_____

_____

Research It

Read the list of ideas from Day 3. Use encyclopedias or the Internet to find out two things that you did not know about each idea. Write the information on the lines. Then share your ideas with a partner.

five-dollar bill

_____

_____

_____

sports car

_____

_____

_____

teachers

_____

_____

_____

Assessment

Read the question. Then complete the chart.

Knowledge Chart

Question	What do I know?	Is this enough information?	What questions do I have?
What is swimming?			

Overview Develop an Outline of Information

Directions and Sample Answers for Activity Pages

Day 1	See "Provide a Real-World Example" below.
Day 2	Read the title and directions aloud. Invite students to read each group of words. Tell students that each group tells, or supports, a big idea about plants. Ask students to think about the words, decide what the big idea is, and write the idea on the line. Then have students share their thinking with a partner. (Answers: parts of a plant, what plants need to live, where plants grow) Finally, ask students to choose one group of words and illustrate it. Have students share their drawings with a partner.
Day 3	Read the title and directions aloud. Invite students to look at the charts. Explain that each chart is about a different part of school. Ask students to complete each chart with three details that support each big idea. Have students share their thinking with a partner. Finally, have students choose one chart and illustrate the information in the chart. (Possible answers: first chart—how to read, how to get along with others, how to write; second chart—books, paper, pencils; third chart—friends, teachers, janitors)
Day 4	Read the title and directions aloud. Invite pairs of students to look at the incomplete chart and fill in the missing information. (Possible answers: blackbirds, vultures, cardinals; where birds build nests; worms, bugs, birdseed)
Day 5	Read the directions aloud. Allow time for students to complete the task. (Possible answers: types of sharks; fish, seals, dolphins; where sharks live) Afterward, meet individually with students. Ask students to share responses with you. Discuss their results. Use their responses to plan further instruction.

Provide a Real-World Example

◆ Hand out the Day 1 activity page. **Say:** *We have learned a lot about writing. Now we are going to learn how to organize information so that we can write things that make sense.*

◆ **Ask:** *What does the word **organize** mean?* (Allow responses.) **Say:** *Yes. **Organize** means to put things in an order that makes sense. When authors write nonfiction, they organize information in a way that makes sense. First they write down big ideas. Then they write details that support the big ideas. We call this plan an outline. I want to write a short paper about bathing a dog. Watch as I organize my information into a chart.* (Use the chart to show students how to organize information.)

◆ **Say:** *The first thing I need to do is write down my big ideas. For bathing a dog, I'm going to choose why dogs need baths, what things are needed for a bath, and how to give a dog a bath. Now I'll fill in the details for each big idea.*

◆ Complete the chart. **Say:** *Wow! I wrote a lot. My next step is to write these ideas into complete sentences and work on my hook and ending. Remember to plan before you write. It makes writing a little easier.*

Bathing a Dog

Big Ideas	Details
why dogs need baths	dogs gets dirty outside, dogs get fleas and fleas can make them sick
what things are needed for a bath	a place to give the dog a bath like a bathtub or big bucket, dog soap, brush or sponge, lots of water, towels to dry off the dog
how to give a bath	1. if inside, close the bathroom door so the dog can't get out, if outside, put the dog on a leash so he can't run away; 2. gently pour water on dog; 3. put soap on the sponge or brush and wash the dog all over; 4. gently wash face; 5. rinse and dry

Develop an Outline of Information

Listen to you teacher. Then complete the chart.

1. Choose an idea—dogs

2. Narrow an idea—bathing a dog

3. Develop an idea—what I know and don't know about bathing a dog

4. Develop an outline—organize information to write

Bathing a Dog

Big Ideas	Details

What's the Big Idea?

Look at each group of words. Each group supports a big idea about plants. Decide what the big idea is and write it on the line. Then share your big ideas with a partner. Explain how you got your answers.

leaves

roots

stems

flowers

Big Idea:

_____

_____

air

light

soil

water

Big Idea:

_____

_____

gardens

forests

beaches

deserts

Big Idea:

_____

_____

Choose one big idea and draw a picture to illustrate it.
Share your drawing with a partner.

Support the Big Idea

Look at the charts. Each chart is about a different part of school.
Three boxes are under each big idea. For each box, write one detail that supports
its big idea. Share your thinking with a partner.

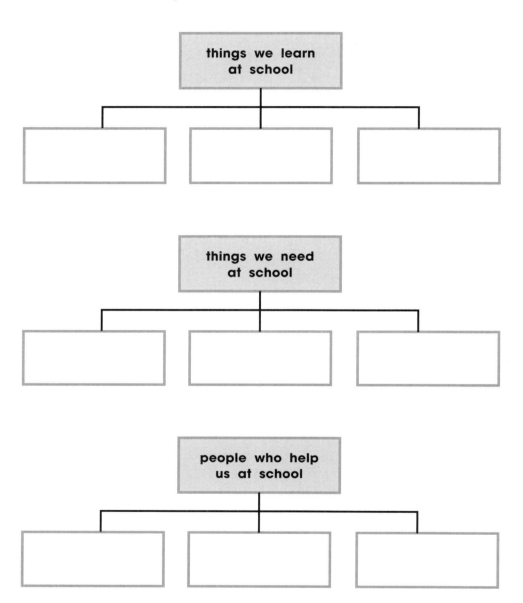

Choose one chart. Draw pictures that explain each detail.

Make an Outline

Look at the chart about birds. Fill in the missing information.

Birds

Big Ideas	Details
kinds of birds	
	in trees, houses, buildings, birdhouses
what birds eat	

Assessment

Look at the chart about sharks. Fill in the missing information.

Sharks

Big Ideas	Details
	hammerhead, great white, nurse, white-tip
what sharks eat	
	warm water, Pacific Ocean, Atlantic Ocean

Overview   Strong Nonfiction Leads

Directions and Sample Answers for Activity Pages

Day 1	See "Provide a Real-World Example" below.
Day 2	Read the title and directions aloud. Invite students to look at the chart and read the leads. Then ask students to analyze the leads and identify which lead they prefer. Finally, have students share their thinking with a partner.
Day 3	Read the title and directions aloud. Invite students to look at the pictures on the left side of the page. Then ask students to match each picture with its correct lead. Ask students to share their results with a partner. (Answers: mountain chain—#4; cat—#5; yard covered in trash—#2; butterfly garden—#3; window—#1) For an extra lesson, help students analyze the different types of leads used in this exercise. (#1—describing a sound; #2—stating an opinion; #3—dialogue; #4—using a single word; #5—using a question)
Day 4	Read the title and directions aloud. Invite students to look at the pictures. Then ask students to write a strong lead for each picture. If students struggle, have them review leads from Day 3 and offer assistance. Ask students to share their results with a partner.
Day 5	Read the directions aloud. Allow time for students to complete the tasks. Afterward, meet individually with students. Discuss their results. Use their responses to plan further instruction.

Provide a Real-World Example

◆ Hand out the Day 1 activity page.

◆ **Say:** *When authors write nonfiction, they begin with a sentence or two that makes readers want to keep reading. We call these sentences strong leads, or hooks. Let's say that I'm going to write about dogs. I've written two leads and can't decide which one to choose.*

◆ Have a student read the leads, and help students analyze them and complete the chart, using the following information.

First Lead:
1. simply states what the author is writing about
2. doesn't offer any information about dogs
3. weak lead

Second Lead:
1. is written in question form
2. offers information about the topic
3. strong lead

◆ **Ask:** *Which lead makes you want to read my paper? Why?* (Allow responses.)

◆ **Say:** *The second lead sounds more interesting than the first. I think my readers will want to read more about dogs. Remember to use a strong lead to hook your reader.*

◆ Remind students that leads like "This paper is about . . ." or "I'm going to tell you about a . . ." are not strong leads.

Nonfiction Leads

Dogs are good pets.	What type of animal has four legs, a wet nose, and lots of energy?
simply states what the author is writing about; doesn't offer any information about dogs; weak lead	is written in question form; offers information about the topic; strong lead

Name _____

Strong Nonfiction Leads

Complete the chart.

Nonfiction Leads

Dogs are good pets.	What type of animal has four legs, a wet nose, and lots of energy?

Strong and Weak Nonfiction Leads

Read the nonfiction leads. Tell which lead is strong and which lead is weak. Explain your thinking on the chart. Answer the question at the bottom of the page and share your thinking with a partner.

Fish Leads

I'm going to tell you about fish.	They may be stinky and slippery, but they taste great.

Which lead do you like better? Why?

_____

_____

Lead Match-Up

Look at the pictures on the left side of the page. Each picture represents a nonfiction writing idea. Read the strong nonfiction leads on the right side of the page. Draw a line from the picture to its matching lead. Share your results with a partner.

Strong Nonfiction Leads

Plink. Plink. Plink.
Ice makes a funny sound when it hits glass.

I think everyone should take care of their own trash.

"Wow!" the girl yelled. "The butterfly garden really did attract butterflies."

Mountains. Their pointed tops reach to the sky.

Have you ever seen anything as cute as a fluffy cat?

Write a Lead

Look at the pictures. Each picture stands for a nonfiction writing idea. Write a strong nonfiction lead for each picture and share your leads with a partner.

_____

_____

_____

_____

Assessment

Read the nonfiction leads. Tell which lead is strong and which lead is weak. Explain what makes each lead strong or weak.

Gum

Gum is a mess.	Gum. Glorious gum. Sticky gum. There has never been a candy so wonderful as gum.

Look at the picture and write a strong nonfiction lead.

_____

_____

_____

Overview Strong Fiction Leads

Directions and Sample Answers for Activity Pages

Day 1	See "Provide a Real-World Example" below.
Day 2	Read the title and directions aloud. Invite students to look at the chart and read the leads. Then ask students to analyze the leads and identify which lead they prefer. Finally, have students share their thinking with a partner.
Day 3	Read the title and directions aloud. Invite students to look at the pictures on the left side of the page. Then ask students to match each picture with its correct lead. Ask students to share their results with a partner. (Answers: mountain chain—#3; little girl snuggling with a cat—#5; yard covered in trash—#1; garden in winter—#2; little boy covered in mud—#4) For an extra lesson, help students analyze the different types of leads used in this exercise. (#1—using a single word; #2—a question; #3—dialogue; #4—describing a sound; #5—telling a fact)
Day 4	Read the title and directions aloud. Invite students to look at the pictures. Then ask students to write a strong lead for each picture. If students struggle, have them review leads from Day 3 and offer assistance. Ask students to share their results with a partner.
Day 5	Read the directions aloud. Allow time for students to complete the tasks. Afterward, meet individually with students. Discuss their results. Use their responses to plan further instruction.

Provide a Real-World Example

◆ Hand out the Day 1 activity page.

◆ **Say:** *When authors write stories, they begin with a sentence or two that makes readers want to keep reading. We call these sentences strong leads, or hooks. Let's say that I'm going to write a story about my dog. I've written two leads and can't decide which one to choose. Look at the leads on the board.*

◆ Have a student read the leads and help students analyze them by completing the chart. Use the information here to guide discussion.

◆ **Ask:** *Which lead makes you want to read my story? Why?* (Allow responses.)

◆ **Say:** *The second lead sounds more interesting than the first. I think my readers will want to find out what happened to the dog. Remember to use a strong lead that hooks readers.*

◆ Remind students that leads like "This story is about . . ." or "I'm going to tell you a story about a . . ." are not strong leads.

Fiction Leads

This story is about my dog.	Rats! That dog got out again.
simply states what the author is writing about; doesn't offer any information about the dog; weak lead	"Rats!" says that the author doesn't like what has happened; "again" says that the dog gets out a lot; the reader might think the dog is a little bit of trouble and wants to see what other trouble the dog gets into; strong lead

Name _____

Strong Fiction Leads

Complete the chart.

Fiction Leads

This story is about my dog.	Rats! That dog got out again.

Unit 6 • Everyday Writing Intervention Activities Grade 3 • © 2011 Newmark Learning, LLC

Strong and Weak Fiction Leads

Read the following story leads. Tell which lead is strong and which lead is weak. Explain your thinking in the space provided. Answer the question at the bottom of the page and share your thinking with a partner.

Fish Leads

Clammy was a clown fish.	Dash! Clammy, the clown fish, darted from one side of the tank to the other.

Which lead do you like better? Why?

_____

_____

Fiction Lead Match-Up

Look at the pictures on the left side of the page. Each picture represents a story. Read the strong fiction leads on the right side of the page. Draw a line from the picture to its matching lead. Share your thinking with a partner.

Strong Fiction Leads

Trash. The whole front yard was covered with trash. But how did it get there?

How could anything that is so pretty in spring look like this in winter?

"Wow!" I shouted. "Are we going to climb that thing?"

Schlop, schlop, schlop. **I wondered what that sound was, and then I saw my little brother.**

The cat was not pretty, but she was so soft.

Write a Lead

Look at the pictures. Each picture stands for a story. Write a strong story lead for each picture and share your leads with a partner.

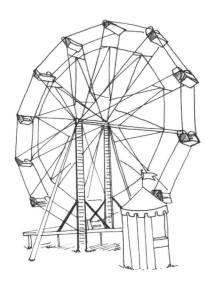

_____

_____

_____

_____

Assessment

Read the following story leads. Tell which lead is strong and which lead is weak. Explain what makes each lead strong or weak.

Gum

I went to bed with gum in my mouth.	What a mess! My mother told me not to do it, but I did it anyway. I went to bed with gum in my mouth. I'll say it again. What a mess.

Look at this picture from a story. Write a strong lead for the story.

_____

_____

Overview Develop a Plot

Directions and Sample Answers for Activity Pages

Day 1	See "Provide a Real-World Example" below.
Day 2	Read the title and directions aloud. Have students share their work with a partner.
Day 3	Read the title and directions aloud. Ask students to complete the stories by drawing the missing event. Have students share their drawings with a partner.
Day 4	Read the title and directions aloud. Have students ask a partner to identify which event was illustrated. (Answers: 6, 2, 4, 3, 1, 5)
Day 5	Read the directions aloud. Allow time for students to complete the tasks. Afterward, meet individually with students. Discuss their results. Use their responses to plan further instruction.

Provide a Real-World Example

◆ Hand out the Day 1 activity page. **Say:** *What makes a story interesting to you?* (Allow responses.) *The things, or events, that happen in a story are called the plot. Good authors spend time planning, or developing, a plot before they start writing. Authors make decisions about time, setting, characters, and the big events that will occur in their story. Watch as I develop the plot for a story.*

◆ **Say:** *The first thing I need to do is decide on my setting, which is time and place. I think the time can be the present time during the fall. It is late afternoon and the sun is setting, so it's getting dark. The place for my story has to be really spooky. I'll choose a forest. The trees have bare branches because the leaves have fallen. The branches look like long, pointy fingers. Maybe I'll also include the weather. It's very windy and chilly. I think the beginning, or introduction, of my story should be two brothers who decide to take a shortcut through a forest on their way home from school. Their mother told them never to do this because they could get lost or get hurt. Now I'll develop the plot for the rest of the story.*

◆ Use the chart to show students how to develop the rest of the plot for the spooky short story. Explain that each event connects to the next event and the problem pushes the story along. Point out that the first event is the problem. What are the boys going to do? The remaining events answer the question. Point out that the fourth event is the resolution to the problem. The boys find out what caused their problem.

◆ **Say:** *The last thing I need to do is decide how my story will end. This is called the conclusion. I think the brothers have learned their lesson. I think they won't go through the woods again, but what if they change their minds? Let me write in my conclusion.*

◆ **Say:** *Remember that this chart just shows my big events and ideas. To write a really good short story, I need to include details about the setting, the brothers, the forest, and the mother. All of these things will keep my readers interested and maybe a little scared.*

Plot Chart

Time	late afternoon/present time; fall; sun is setting
Place	a spooky forest with trees that have bare branches; weather is windy and chilly
Introduction	two brothers take a shortcut on the way home from school
Plot (Story Events)	1. boys hear terrible sounds and feel something scratching them 2. boys run through the forest until they get to their house 3. the brothers do not tell their mother—they are scared to death 4. later that evening, their mother tells them that she knew they had walked through the forest and tricked them
Conclusion	the brothers have learned their lesson and will never go through the forest again . . . maybe

Name _____

Develop a Plot

Complete the plot chart.

Plot Chart

Time	
Place	
Introduction	
Plot (Story Events)	
Conclusion	

Draw a Setting

Think of a story idea that you might like to write about. Where does your story take place? What does the setting look like? In the space below, use crayons, pencils, and/or markers to draw your setting. Remember that the more details you include, the better your drawing and writing will be.

What Happened?

Read the stories. For each story, an event is missing. Draw the missing events in the boxes. Share your drawings with a partner.

Story #1

First event

One day, Annie went to the park. She sat on a bench and ate peanuts. After a while, she laid the peanut bag on the bench and ran to the playground.

Second event

Third event

Annie came back to the bench and found her peanut bag, but the peanuts were gone. Where could they have gone? She looked around and saw a plump squirrel. Hmm.

Story #2

First event

Spike, the dog, runs outside to play in his backyard. He notices chickens in the neighbor's yard.

Second event

Third event

"Come inside," yells Spike's owner. Spike runs inside with a feather hanging out of his mouth. "Uh oh," the owner whispers. "What did you do?"

Plot Order

The story below is about a cat named Seymour. Read the story events. They are out of order. Order the events from 1 to 6. Share your thinking with a partner.

☐   The kitten climbed up the tree and helped Seymour climb down the tree.

☐   Seymour chased a kitten up a tree.

☐   A fireman got the kitten out of the tree, but not Seymour.

☐   Seymour followed the kitten up the tree and got caught.

☐   Seymour, the cat, spent every afternoon chasing other cats up trees.

☐   It started to rain, and Seymour got soaked.

Choose one event and draw a picture of it in the space below. Ask a partner to choose which event you drew.

Name _____

Assessment

Read the plot chart. Some information is missing. Complete the chart.

Plot Chart

Time	8:30 in the morning
Place	the beach
Introduction	
Story Events (Plot)	1. Mary and Jack play in the water and sand. Their mother tells them not to pick up the hermit crabs because they will pinch. 2. Mary tells Jack that hermit crabs won't really pinch. Mom was just kidding. 3. Jack picks up a hermit crab and places it in the palm of his hand.
Conclusion	

Read the story events. An event is missing. Draw the missing event in the box provided.

First event

Michael and Tyler play together on the school's playground.

Second event

Third event

Michael and Tyler end up at the bottom of the slide in a pile.

Overview   Develop a Character

Directions and Sample Answers for Activity Pages

Day 1	See "Provide a Real-World Example" below.
Day 2	Read the title and directions aloud. Invite students to look at the pictures and read the matching problems. Then ask them to draw how the character changes after the problem occurs. Finally, have students share their drawings with a partner.
Day 3	Read the title and directions aloud. Invite students to look at the two sets of character pictures. Ask students what they think might have happened to change the character. Then ask them to write their ideas on the lines in the middle of the two pictures. Finally, have students share their thinking with a partner.
Day 4	Read the title and directions aloud. Invite students to look at the character webs. To the side of each web, ask students to draw pictures of how Tom changes. Remind students to think about how Tom changes over time. Have students share their drawings with a partner.
Day 5	Read the directions aloud. Allow time for students to complete the task. Afterward, meet individually with students. Discuss their results. Use their responses to plan further instruction.

Provide a Real-World Example

◆ Hand out the Day 1 activity page. **Say:** *Characters are the most important part of a story. Good writers plan their characters before writing. They decide what characters will look like and how they will act. These are called character traits. Then as the story develops, so do the characters. They may keep the same traits or change traits because of story events.*

◆ **Say:** *This is a character chart for Ann. She's in a story I want to write. I want Ann to be the heroine in the story. She tells the truth, is kind to everyone, and tries hard with her schoolwork. When I write my story, I'll be sure to include all of these traits and include details that support my character traits about Ann.* (Complete the first character web.)

◆ **Say:** *I want my story to be interesting, so I need something to happen . . . I need a problem. Maybe my problem is that Ann has trouble one day in math class and gets a bad grade on a test. This event causes her actions to change. Help me change Ann in the second character web.*

◆ Help students revise Ann to match the problem. Use information in the second web to develop Ann's character. **Say:** *I need to keep my story moving, so I need the problem to be resolved. Maybe Ann's mother finds the test paper after Ann has lied about it. Ann's mom talks to Ann about what she's done, and helps Ann learn a life lesson. Let's change Ann one more time to match that event.* Help students revise Ann to match the resolution. Use information in the third web to redefine Ann's character.

◆ **Say:** *We must remember that a character's actions match what is happening in the story. For a character to develop, the author keeps both character and story events in mind when writing.*

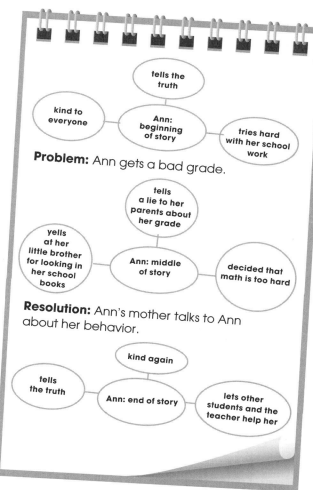

Problem: Ann gets a bad grade.

Resolution: Ann's mother talks to Ann about her behavior.

Develop a Character

Complete the character webs.

Problem: Ann gets a bad grade on her math test.

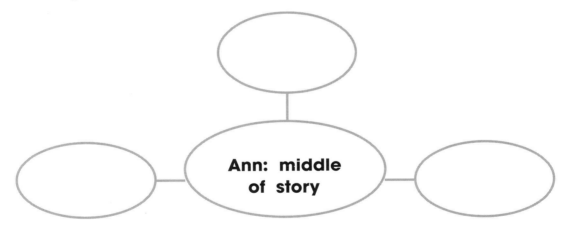

Resolution: Ann's mother talks to Ann about her behavior and tells her to always tell the truth, no matter what.

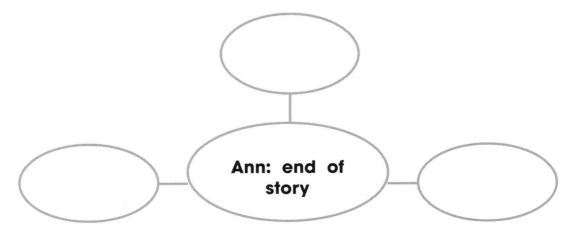

Character Changes

Look at the pictures and read the matching problems. Draw how you think the problem might change the character. Share your drawings with a partner.

Problem: Another child takes the boy's toy away from him.

Problem: The soccer ball hits another child on the shoulder.

What Happened?

Look at the two sets of character pictures. What do you think might have happened to change the character? Write your ideas between the pictures. Share your thoughts with a partner.

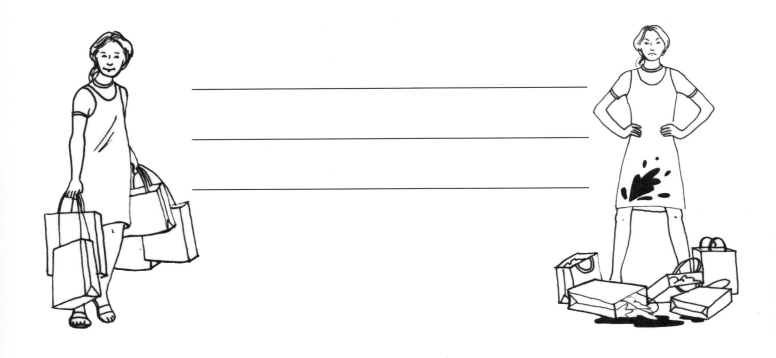

_____

_____

_____

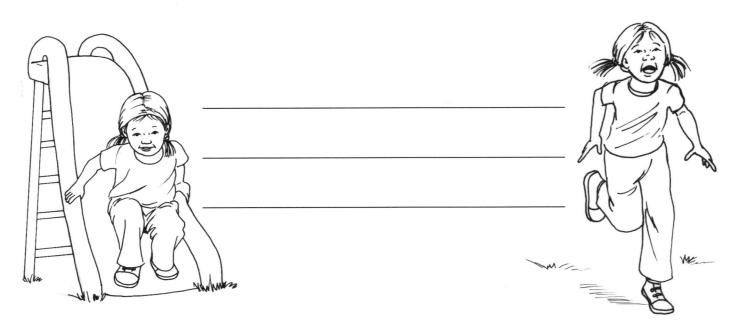

_____

_____

_____

Develop a Character

Look at the character webs. They tell how a character named Tom changes in a story. Think about how each web describes Tom. For each web, draw pictures that show what you think Tom looks like. Share your thinking with a partner.

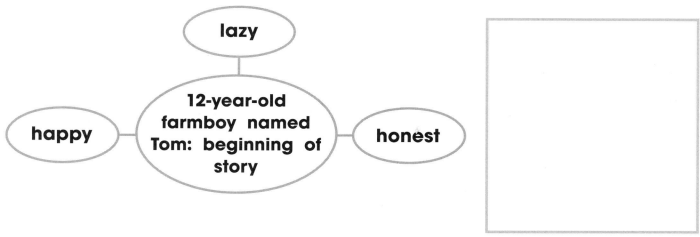

Problem: Tom sneaks an apple from his neighbor's barn.

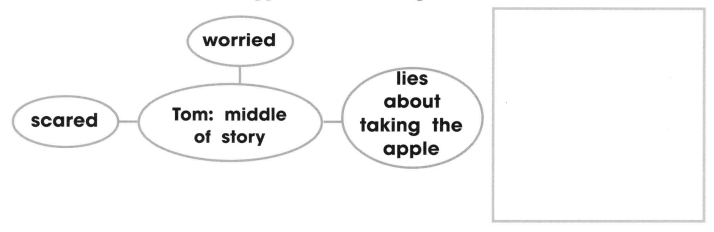

Resolution: Tom gets caught with the apple in his pocket.

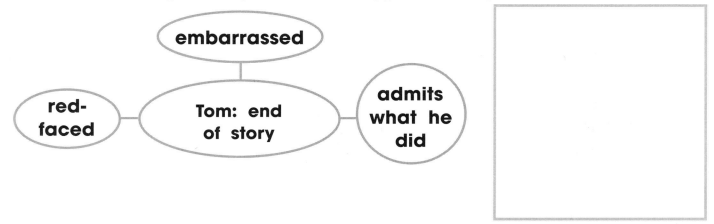

Assessment

Read the first character web. Use it to develop the same character in the other character webs.

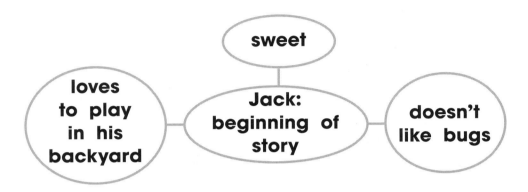

Problem: Jack gets stung by a bee in his backyard.

Resolution: Jack's parents take him to a museum where he sees all kinds of bugs. He learns that bugs are a part of nature.

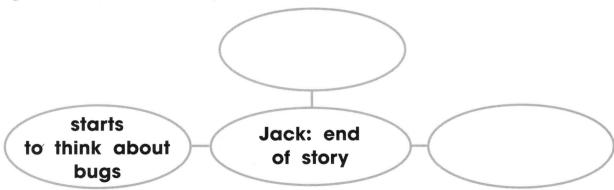

Overview Strong Nonfiction Endings

Directions and Sample Answers for Activity Pages

Day 1	See "Provide a Real-World Example" below.
Day 2	Read the title and directions aloud. Invite students to look at the chart and read the endings. Then ask students to analyze the endings and identify which ending they prefer. Finally, have students share their thinking with a partner.
Day 3	Read the title and directions aloud. Invite students to look at the pictures on the left side of the page. Then ask students to match each picture with its correct ending. Ask students to share their results with a partner. (Answers: trashy park—#4; George Washington—#1; grocery bags—#5; moon—#2; butterfly—#3) For an extra lesson, help students analyze the different types of endings used in this exercise. (#1 and 2—restate an important idea; #3—summarize information; #4—call to action; #5—change way of thinking)
Day 4	Read the title and directions aloud. Invite students to look at the pictures. Then ask students to write a strong ending for each picture. If students struggle, have them review endings from Day 3 and offer assistance. Ask students to share their results with a partner.
Day 5	Read the directions aloud. Allow time for students to complete the tasks. Afterward, meet individually with students. Discuss their results. Use their responses to plan further instruction.

Provide a Real-World Example

◆ Hand out the Day 1 activity page. **Say:** *When authors write nonfiction, they begin with a sentence or two that makes readers want to keep reading. We call these sentences strong leads, or hooks. They also want to end with sentences that keep their readers thinking.*

◆ **Say:** *Let's say that I'm going to write about penguins. I've written two endings and can't decide which one to choose. Look at the endings on the board.*

◆ Have one student read the endings and help students analyze them and complete the chart using the chart here.

◆ **Ask:** *Which ending makes you think about how amazing penguins really are? Why?* (Allow responses.)

◆ **Say:** *The second ending sounds more interesting than the first. I think my readers will think about penguins because I added some of the things they do. I sort of summarized their actions. Remember to use a strong ending to help your readers think.*

◆ Remind students that endings like "This paper was about . . ." or "These _____ are wonderful." are not strong endings.

Nonfiction Endings

Penguins are interesting animals.	They swim, jump, and waddle. They do everything but fly. Penguins are nature's amazing animals.
simply states what the author has written about; doesn't offer any information about penguins; weak ending	summarizes what is so amazing about penguins; offers information about penguins; strong ending

Strong Nonfiction Endings

Complete the chart.

Nonfiction Endings

Penguins are interesting animals.	They swim, jump, and waddle. They do everything but fly. Penguins are nature's amazing animals.

Strong and Weak Nonfiction Endings

Read the nonfiction endings. Tell which ending is strong and which ending is weak. Explain your thinking. Answer the question at the bottom of the page and share your thinking with a partner.

T. Rex

T. rex was the most dangerous dinosaur ever.	T. rex had sharp claws, sharp teeth, a huge body, and a huge tail. What animal wouldn't be afraid?

Which ending do you like better? Why?

_____

Ending Match-Up

Look at the pictures on the left side of the page. Each picture stands for a nonfiction writing idea. Read the nonfiction endings on the right side of the page. Draw a line from the picture to its matching ending. Share your results with a partner.

Strong Nonfiction Endings

George Washington was a great man because he could lead people.

The moon is thousands of miles away, but it still makes us wonder.

Butterflies come in all sizes and colors, and they are all beautiful.

We have the power to solve our dirty park problem. Stand with me today.

Cloth grocery bags do cost a little bit of money, but isn't Earth worth it?

Name _____

Write an Ending

Look at the pictures. Each picture stands for a nonfiction writing idea. Write a strong nonfiction ending for each picture and share your endings with a partner.

_____

_____

_____

_____

Assessment

Read the nonfiction endings. Tell which ending is strong and which ending is weak. Explain what makes each ending strong or weak.

Baseball

I think kids should be able to play baseball.	All kids should have the chance to play baseball. Won't you help us rebuild our field?

Look at the picture and write a strong nonfiction ending.

_____

_____

_____

Overview Strong Fiction Endings

Directions and Sample Answers for Activity Pages

Day 1	See "Provide a Real-World Example" below.
Day 2	Read the title and directions aloud. Invite students to look at the chart and read the endings. Then ask students to analyze the endings and identify which ending they prefer. Have students share their thinking with a partner.
Day 3	Read the title and directions aloud. Invite students to look at the pictures on the left side of the page. Then ask students to match each picture with its correct ending. Ask students to share their results with a partner. (Answers: bunny family—#3; lost kitten—#5; two girls sitting at pond—#1; boy with frog and whistle—#2; volcano boy—#4) For an extra lesson, help students analyze the different types of endings used in this exercise. (#1—look towards the future; #2—humor; #3—restating an important idea in the story; #4—life goes on; #5—personal observation)
Day 4	Read the title and directions aloud. Invite students to look at the pictures. Then ask students to write a strong ending for each picture. If students struggle, have them review endings from Day 3 and offer assistance. Ask students to share their results with a partner.
Day 5	Read the directions aloud. Allow time for students to complete the tasks. Afterward, meet individually with students. Discuss their results. Use their responses to plan further instruction.

Provide a Real-World Example

◆ Hand out the Day 1 activity page. **Say:** *When authors write stories, they begin with a sentence or two that makes readers want to keep reading. We call these sentences strong leads, or hooks. Authors also want to end with sentences that keep their readers thinking.*

◆ **Say:** *Let's say that I have written a story about a girl named Mary. She's had a terrible day. One thing after another went wrong. I've written two endings and can't decide which one to choose. Look at the endings on the board.*

◆ Have one student read the endings. Help students analyze them and complete the chart. **Ask:** *Which ending makes you think? Why?* (Allow responses.)

◆ **Say:** *The second ending sounds more interesting than the first. The second ending reminds me of what happened to Mary. It also helps me remember that tomorrow is always another day. Just because bad things happen on one day does not mean that good things can't happen the next day.*

◆ Remind students that endings like "My story is done." or "This is the end of my story." are not strong endings.

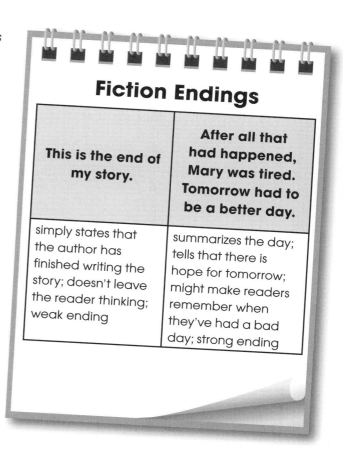

Fiction Endings

This is the end of my story.	After all that had happened, Mary was tired. Tomorrow had to be a better day.
simply states that the author has finished writing the story; doesn't leave the reader thinking; weak ending	summarizes the day; tells that there is hope for tomorrow; might make readers remember when they've had a bad day; strong ending

Strong Fiction Endings

Complete the chart.

Fiction Endings

This is the end of my story.	After all that had happened, Mary was tired. Tomorrow had to be a better day.

Strong and Weak Fiction Endings

These endings complete a story about two boys who like to play marble games and nothing else. Read the endings. Tell which ending is strong and which ending is weak. Explain your thinking on the chart. Answer the question at the bottom of the page and share your thinking with a partner.

Just Marbles

Jack and Sam decided to play with other toys for the rest of the day.	Marbles were fun, but other toys could be just as fun. Maybe the boys would play marbles tomorrow. Then again, maybe not.

Which ending do you like better? Why?

_____

Story Ending Match-Up

Look at the pictures on the left side of the page. Each picture represents a story. Read the strong endings on the right side of the page. Draw a line from the picture to its matching ending. Share your results with a partner.

Strong Fiction Endings

Tammy did not know what would happen on Friday, but Ann would be there, too.

And there was George holding a frog in one hand and a whistle in the other hand. What a goof.

"But the best part of life," thought the bunny, "was having family."

"I don't have time to think about it right now," answered Sam. "I have a volcano to make."

Once in a great while, things worked out. Sally turned and carried her kitten home.

Unit 10 • Everyday Writing Intervention Activities Grade 3 • © 2011 Newmark Learning, LLC

Write an Ending

Look at the pictures. Each picture stands for a story. Write a strong ending for each picture and share them with a partner.

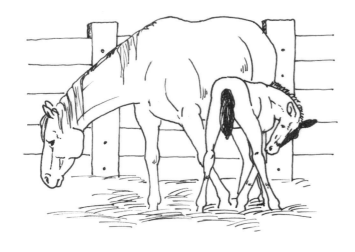

_____

_____

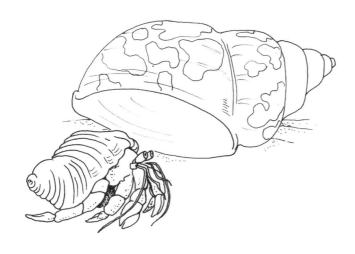

_____

_____

Assessment

Read the story endings. Tell which ending is strong and which ending is weak. Explain what makes each ending strong or weak.

The Trip

We came home on Friday.	At five o'clock on Friday afternoon, we finally got home. It had been a long, fun trip to the beach. We couldn't wait until next year's vacation.

Look at this picture from a story. Write a strong ending for the story.

_____

_____

Overview What Is Voice?

Directions and Sample Answers for Activity Pages

Day 1	See "Provide a Real-World Example" below.
Day 2	Read the title and directions aloud. Invite students to read the sentences. Ask students to act out how they might really say each sentence. Ask students to choose one sentence and write it as they said it in their own voice.
Day 3	Read the title and directions aloud. Invite students to read the scenes. Ask student pairs to act out what might happen in the scene and record the dialogue. If time allows, have student pairs act out one scene for the group.
Day 4	Read the title and directions aloud. Ask students to draw lines from each cartoon to its matching caption. Then have students look at the cartoon at the bottom of the page and write a caption. (Answer: tree and squirrel—#4; cat—#1; frogs—#2; dog chasing tail—#3)
Day 5	Read the directions aloud. Allow time for students to complete the tasks. Afterward, meet individually with students. Discuss their results. Use their responses to plan further instruction.

Provide a Real-World Example

◆ Hand out the Day 1 activity page. **Say:** *Turn to your neighbor and read the first sentence.* Allow time for students to read the sentence. **Say:** *Now say the sentence again, but this time, say it like you are really trying to talk your mom into letting you go to John's party.* Allow time for students to read the sentence. Then talk about the differences. **Say:** *When we write, we want our words to sound like the way we would really speak. This is called voice. Think about how you would ask your mother to go to a birthday party. What do you do with the sound of your voice? How do you say the words? Are you going to use a loud voice or a soft voice? Are you going to say something that might make her mad?*

◆ **Say:** *When you read the sentence the second time, I knew you were not simply reading it. I knew which child was saying the sentence a certain way. I heard your voices. The way we speak is most often the best way to write. But how would I write that sentence to show my voice coming through? Watch as I rewrite the sentence.*

◆ Rewrite the sentence on the board. **Ask:** *Now look at the sentence. I changed the way **please** looks, and I would not count that as a spelling mistake. I even added a few more pleases. I also added an extra sentence that might help my mom understand why I want to go to the party so badly. This sounds more like how you all sounded. I wrote the sentence in your voice.*

◆ Repeat the process with the remaining sentences.

What is Voice?

Mom, may I please go to John's birthday party?

Mom, may I pleeeeease go over to John's birthday party? Please. Please. Pretty please. It will be so much fun, and everyone will be there.

The dog ran up the tree.

That dog ran up the tree again. Can you believe it?

The wind is blowing my hair.

The wind is blowing my haaaiiirr in my eyes. I can't see a thing!

The flowers were beautiful. I don't mind staying in my room now.

The flowers were beautiful. Now I don't mind being cooped up in my bedroom.

Voice

Rewrite the sentences using voice.

1. Mom, may I go please go to John's birthday party?

_____

_____

2. The dog ran up the tree.

_____

_____

3. The wind is blowing my hair.

_____

_____

4. The flowers were beautiful. I don't mind staying in my room now.

_____

_____

Act It Out

Read the sentences as they are written. With a partner, act out how you might say them in real life.

My brother can be mean.

That game costs a lot of money.

I need to take a nap.

Please stop making that noise!

Choose one sentence. Say it again using voice. Write the sentence as you said it. Remember that you can change the way words are spelled and how they look.

_____

_____

Other Voices

Look at the scenes. With your partner, act out a short conversation that might happen between the two objects. Record the dialogue.

1. a sock talking to a stinky shoe

_____

_____

_____

2. a chalkboard talking to a piece of chalk

_____

_____

_____

3. a paintbrush talking to paint

_____

_____

_____

4. a football talking to a football shoe

_____

_____

_____

Voice Bubbles

Draw a line from the cartoon to its matching caption.

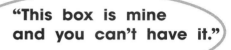

"This box is mine and you can't have it."

"I told you not to eat that fly."

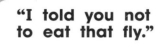

"I can't believe it's come to this. I'm chasing my own tail and I like it."

"You're tickling me. Stop it. Stop it. Please STOP IT."

Look at the cartoon. What would you say if you were one of the characters in the cartoon? Write a caption that shows voice.

_____

_____

Assessment

Read the sentences. Say them to yourself using your voice. Write the sentence as you said it. Remember that you can change the way words are spelled and the way they look.

I don't want to go to the store.

_____

_____

Can I sleep a little longer?

_____

_____

Look at the scenes. Choose one and write a caption for it. Remember to think about what you might say if you were the animal in the cartoon.

_____   _____

Overview Using Different Voices

Directions and Sample Answers for Activity Pages

Day 1	See "Provide a Real-World Example" below.
Day 2	Read the title and directions aloud. Invite students to read the sentences. Then ask students to think about the audience. Is it the principal or a friend? Tell students to put a P for principal or an F for friend. Have students share their answers with a partner. (Answers: 1. P; 2. F; 3. F; 4. P; 5. P; 6. F) Then have students construct the sentences at the bottom of the page. Remind students to remember their audience.
Day 3	Read the title and directions aloud. Invite students to read the sentences and to think about who might say the sentences and to write their answers on the lines provided. Finally, have students act out how each person they suggested might say the sentence.
Day 4	Read the title and directions aloud. Invite students to read the sentences in the left column. Then ask students to read the words in the right column. Ask students to think about who the audience for each sentence might be. Have students draw a line matching the sentence on the left with its corresponding audience on the right. Have students share their results with a partner. (Answers: 1. a teacher; 2. a celebrity; 3. your neighbor; 4. a toy company; 5. a friend; 6. a school cook) Finally, have students choose one sentence and illustrate it.
Day 5	Read the directions aloud. Allow time for students to complete the tasks. (Answers: 1. your mother; 2. a teacher; 3. your dog; 4. a friend) Afterward, meet individually with students. Discuss their results. Use their responses to plan further instruction.

Provide a Real-World Example

◆ Hand out the Day 1 activity page. Write on the board the two short letters from the Day 1 handout. **Ask:** *How do you speak to a friend? How do you speak to an adult? Do you sound the same? Do you use the same words? No. You probably change the way you speak. We do that when we talk. The way you sound when you talk is called voice. We use different voices when we write, too. A letter to a friend looks different than a letter to the school principal. Look at the short letters on the board.* Have a student read the letters. Then discuss the differences.

◆ **Say:** *These letters are both thank-yous, but they are written to different types of people so they should sound different. This is an example of using different voices for different audiences. What is an audience?* (Allow responses.)

◆ **Say:** *An audience is someone who is watching you perform. An audience might watch you perform in a dance recital, a karate match, a soccer game, or a play. An audience is also the person who reads what you write. Writing audiences can be a friend, a principal, a parent or grandparent, a teacher, or even the president of the United States. Remember your audience when you write so that you will use the right voice.*

Different Voices for Different Audiences

letter to a friend	letter to a principal
says the person's name, uses everyday language, does not describe, signed with the writer's name, sounds friendly	starts with "Dear," is a little longer, retells what the principal did, uses very nice language, signed with "Sincerely," sounds like you are talking to an adult (formal)

Name _____

Different Voices for Different Audiences

Complete the chart.

Different Voices for Different Audiences

letter to a friend	letter to a principal

Alan,

Thanks for coming over today. I had a great time. Can't wait for you to come over again.

Johnny

Dear Mr. Jones,

Thank you for coming to our classroom. I liked hearing what your life was like when you were a kid. You were very kind to give up your time for us.

Sincerely,
Johnny Salena

Different Voices, Same Person

Read the sentences. Decide if you would say them to your school's principal or to your friend. Write P for principal and F for friend. Share your answers with a partner.

☐ 1. Yes, sir. I'll be sure to tell my mother what you said.

☐ 2. Okay. I'll tell my mom what you said.

☐ 3. Whoopee! I didn't want to go to the science fair on Saturday anyway.

☐ 4. I'm sorry, but I can't go to the science fair on Saturday.

☐ 5. Yes. I finished my homework and helped clean the classroom.

☐ 6. I finished my homework and then I had to help clean the room. Yuck!

Write a sentence telling your principal that you are sick.

_____

_____

Write a sentence telling your friend that you are sick.

_____

_____

Voice Choice

Read the sentences. First write down two people who might say the sentence. Then act out the sentence with your partner. Be sure to use voice when you act out the sentences.

1. Don't bounce the ball in the house.

Who might say this sentence to you? _____

Who else might say this sentence? _____

2. That bee is going to sting you.

Who might say this sentence to you? _____

Who else might say this sentence? _____

3. Be sure to cross the road at the crosswalk.

Who might say this sentence to you? _____

Who else might say this sentence? _____

4. I want you to help me change the oil in the car.

Who might say this sentence to you? _____

Who else might say this sentence? _____

5. Pick up your toys.

Who might say this sentence to you? _____

Who else might say this sentence? _____

Who's the Audience?

Read the sentences and the audiences. Draw a line from each sentence to its matching audience. Share your answers with a partner.

Sentences	**Audience**
1. Please forgive me for not turning in my homework.	**a school cook**
2. You are the coolest dancer ever.	**a toy company**
3. I am a hard worker and would like to mow your yard this summer.	**a teacher**
4. I don't think you should sell toys that break.	**a celebrity**
5. Can I borrow a piece of paper? I left mine at home.	**a friend**
6. That lunch was the best I've ever eaten.	**your neighbor**

Choose one sentence. Draw a picture that includes the audience. Share your picture with a friend.

Assessment

Write a sentence that matches the scene. Remember to use the right voice for the audience.

Tell your friend you can't come over after school.

_____

Thank your grandmother for a birthday gift.

_____

Read the audiences in the word bank. Match each audience to the correct sentence. Write your answer on the line.

your dog	a teacher	a friend	your mother

1. Tim left the front door open again.

_____

2. Yes, I put the glue tubes and glitter back in the cabinet.

_____

3. You are such a sweet girl. Yes, you are. Yes, you are. Yes, you are.

_____

4. I just ran ten laps, and Coach wants me to run ten more.
   He's driving me nuts.

_____

Overview Adjectives

Directions and Sample Answers for Activity Pages

Day 1	See "Provide a Real-World Example" below.
Day 2	Read the title and directions aloud. Invite students to read the sentences. Then ask them to illustrate what the sentences tell them. Have students share illustrations with a partner.
Day 3	Read the title and directions aloud. Invite students to read the words in the word bank and look at the illustrations. Have students talk about the illustrations with a partner. Then ask students to choose two adjectives from the word bank describing each illustration and write them on the line provided. Finally, have students choose one illustration and write a sentence that includes their adjective choices. (Answers: #1—sleeping, sunny; #2—little, messy; #3—two, scary)
Day 4	Read the title and directions aloud. Invite students to read the sentences. Ask students to revise the sentences by adding at least one adjective to each sentence. Have students share their revised sentences with a partner.
Day 5	Read the directions aloud. Allow time for students to complete the tasks. Afterward, meet individually with students. Discuss their results. Use their responses to plan further instruction.

Provide a Real-World Example

◆ Hand out the Day 1 activity page. **Say:** *Authors want their words to be interesting. They want to create pictures in the minds of their readers. Using adjectives is one way to do this. Adjectives give information about nouns and pronouns. They explain how things look and feel or the size and shape of something.*

◆ **Say:** *Look at the sentences. Are they interesting? Not really. They simply say that spiders have eight legs and make webs to catch food. The facts are true, but not very interesting to read. By adding a few adjectives, I can make the sentences more interesting to read.*

◆ Write the following revised sentences on the board:

Spiders crawl around on eight, crooked legs. They make sticky webs that catch food.

◆ **Say:** *Now look at the sentences. I included the words **crooked** and **sticky**. Each adjective describes something particular. **Crooked** describes what spider legs look like. **Sticky** describes what spider webs feel like. I can really see this spider. Are these sentences more interesting to you? How? (Allow responses.)*

◆ **Say:** *Look at the first two sentences again. What adjectives would you include to make these sentences more interesting? (Allow responses.) Remember, authors want readers to see what they write. Adjectives help do this.*

Using Adjectives

Spiders have eight legs. They make webs that catch food.

Spiders crawl around on eight, crooked legs. They make sticky webs that catch food.

Name _____

Adjectives

Rewrite the sentences to include adjectives.

Spiders have eight legs. They make webs that catch food.

_____

_____

_____

Picture This

Read the sentences. Draw a picture of what the sentence says.

1. Flaky snow fell on a tree's bare branches.

2. Mom poured lumpy pancake batter into the hot frying pan.

3. The sizzling slide burned my legs.

Describing Objects

Look at the pictures. Talk about them with a partner. Then choose two adjectives from the word bank that describe each picture. Write them on the line provided. Share your adjectives with your partner.

little	two	sleeping
scary	sunny	messy

_____

_____

_____

_____

_____

_____

Choose one picture and write a sentence about it. Be sure to include your adjectives. Share your sentence with your partner.

_____

_____

Using Adjectives

Read the sentences. Revise each sentence by adding at least one adjective. Share your revised sentences with a partner.

1. The tree fell.

_____

_____

2. My cat scratched me.

_____

_____

3. Dirt stuck to my foot.

_____

_____

Assessment

Read the sentences. Make changes by adding one adjective to each sentence.

1. We saw _____ bones in the museum.

2. I found an old book in my grandmother's _____ attic.

3. I was happy when I won _____ place.

Look at the picture. Write a sentence that describes the picture. Be sure to use at least one adjective in your sentence.

_____

_____

    Unit 13 • Everyday Writing Intervention Activities Grade 3 • © 2011 Newmark Learning, LLC

Overview Adverbs

Directions and Sample Answers for Activity Pages

Day 1	See "Provide a Real-World Example" below.
Day 2	Read the title and directions aloud. Invite students to read the sentences. Then ask them to illustrate what the sentences tell them. Have students share illustrations with a partner.
Day 3	Read the title and directions aloud. Invite students to read the words in the word bank and look at the illustrations. Have students talk about the illustrations with a partner. Then ask students to choose an **-ly** adverb from the word bank describing each illustration and write it on the line provided. Finally, have students choose one illustration and write a sentence that includes their adverb choice. (Answers: #1—carefully; #2—softly; #3—easily; #4—sadly)
Day 4	Read the title and directions aloud. Invite students to read the sentences. Then ask students to revise the sentences by including one adverb. Have students share revised sentences with a partner. Finally, have students choose one sentence and illustrate it.
Day 5	Read the directions aloud. Allow time for students to complete the tasks. (Answers: #1—quickly; #2—yesterday; #3—inside) Afterward, meet individually with students. Discuss their results. Use their responses to plan further instruction.

Provide a Real-World Example

◆ Hand out the Day 1 activity page. **Say:** *Authors want their words to be interesting. They want to create pictures in the minds of the readers. Using adverbs is one way to do this. Adverbs give information about verbs, adjectives, and other adverbs. They explain how, when, and where something happens.*

◆ **Say:** *Let's rewrite this sentence to include adverbs. The first question is how I painted the picture. Maybe I wanted to take my time, so I painted it slowly. Most adverbs that tell "how" end in -ly.*

◆ Write the following revised sentence on the board: *I slowly painted a picture.* Underline **slowly**.

◆ **Say:** *The second question is when I painted the picture. I'll choose* **yesterday***.*

◆ Write the following revised sentence on the board: *Yesterday I slowly painted a picture.* Underline **yesterday**.

◆ **Say:** *The final question is where I painted the picture. I'll choose* **outside** *because my mother never liked me to paint in the house.*

◆ Write the following revised sentence on the board: *Yesterday I slowly painted a picture outside.* Underline **outside**.

◆ **Ask:** *See how adverbs give more information? Now look at the underlined adverbs. What adverbs would you choose to tell how, when, and where?* Review each sentence and ask students what "how," "when," and "where" adverbs they might choose. (Allow responses.) **Say:** *Remember, authors want to be clear about how, when, and where things are done. Adverbs help do this.*

Using Adverbs

I painted a picture.

I slowly painted a picture.

Yesterday I slowly painted a picture.

Yesterday I slowly painted a picture outside.

Adverbs

Rewrite the sentence to include adverbs.

I painted a picture.

_____

_____

_____

Picture This

Read the sentences. Below each sentence draw a picture of what it tells you.

1. I sat quietly in my grandmother's lap. **("how" adverb)**

2. I'll clean my room tomorrow. It's not that dirty. **("when" adverb)**

3. A rat just ran downstairs to the basement. **("where" adverb)**

-*ly* Adverbs

Look at the pictures. Talk about them with a partner. Then choose the -ly adverb from the word bank that describes each picture. Write the adverb on the line.

softly	easily	sadly	carefully

_____

_____

_____

_____

Choose one picture and write a sentence about it. Be sure to include your adverb. Share your sentence with your partner.

_____

_____

Using Adverbs

Read the sentences. Revise the sentences by adding adverbs that tell how, when, or where. Share your revised sentences with a partner. Choose one sentence and draw what you think it looks like.

1. The dog barked _____. (**"how" adverb ending in –ly**)

_____

_____

2. I have dance class _____. (**"when" adverb**)

_____

_____

3. I climbed _____ to the attic. (**"where" adverb**)

_____

_____

Assessment

Read the following sentences. Then choose an adverb from the word bank and write it on the line provided.

inside	quickly	yesterday

1. We _____ changed into our swimming suits.
("how" adverb)

2. We swam _____ afternoon. **("when" adverb)**

3. The hotel swimming pool was _____ on the third floor. **("where" adverb)**

Look at the picture. Write a sentence telling how something is done. Remember, adverbs telling how usually end in –ly.

_____

_____

Overview Strong Verbs

Directions and Sample Answers for Activity Pages

Day 1	See "Provide a Real-World Example" below.
Day 2	Read the title and directions aloud. With a partner, invite students to read the sentence pairs. Have students act out sentence pairs and decide which sentence contains the strong verb. Have students circle the sentence containing the strong verb. (Answers: 1. begged; 2. built; 3. bounced; 4. Treat) Extra activity: Have pairs choose one strong verb sentence to act out during whole-class time. Have the class identify which sentence the pair acts out.
Day 3	Read the title and directions aloud. Invite students to read the words in the word bank and the sentences. Have students choose the strong verb that completes each sentence and write it on the line provided. Finally, have students choose one sentence and illustrate it. (Answers: #1—replied; #2—bragged; #3—ordered; #4—cried; #5—laughed)
Day 4	Read the title and directions aloud. Invite students to read the words in each column. Then ask students to draw a line from the weak verb to its matching strong verb. Have students choose one strong verb and use it in a sentence. (Answers: give—serve; knock—tackle; tell—describe; fight—argue; make—create)
Day 5	Read the directions aloud. Allow time for students to complete the tasks. (Answers: #1—booed; #2—slithered; #3—joked) Afterward, meet individually with students. Discuss their results. Use their responses to plan further instruction.

Provide a Real-World Example

◆ Hand out the Day 1 activity page. **Say:** *The English language is filled with action words. Action words are called verbs. When we write, we want to use the verb that best describes what is happening. The best verb helps the reader "see" what is happening. Look at the first sentence. There is nothing wrong with the word "ran," but it is a common word. Other words might better describe what the cat is doing, such as* **dashed**, **rushed**, *and* **raced**.

◆ Write the following revised sentence on the board. Underline **dashed**.

My cat dashed across the room.

◆ **Ask:** *Have you ever seen a cat just take off across the room for no reason? That's what* **dashing** *looks like. The word* **dashing** *really shows us what the cat is doing. We could have also used* **raced** *or* **rushed** *in the sentence. Any of these words would have given us a better picture of the cat's action.*

◆ Repeat with the other sentences using strong verbs like **lounges/relaxes** and **snoozes/slumbers**.

◆ **Say:** *Remember, strong verbs really show readers what is happening. Use strong verbs when you write.*

Using Strong Verbs

My cat **ran** across the room.

My cat **dashed** across the room.

My cat **raced** across the room.

My cat **rushed** across the room.

My cat **hurried** across the room.

My cat **scurried** across the room.

Strong Verbs

Rewrite the following sentences to include strong verbs.

My cat ran across the room.

_____

_____

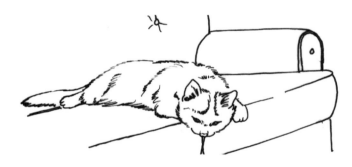

My cat lies on the couch.

_____

_____

My cat sleeps all day long.

_____

_____

Act It Out!

Read each sentence pair. Act out each sentence and decide which one has the strong verb in it. Circle the sentence with the strong verb.

1. Tom asked his dad for an allowance.

   Tom begged his dad for an allowance.

2. Mary built the castle out of trash.

   Mary put the castle together out of trash.

3. The twins jumped around the room.

   The twins bounced around the room.

4. Treat everyone nicely.

   Be nice to everyone.

"Said" Verbs

There are many ways to say "said." Read the sentences. Choose a word from the word bank to complete each sentence. Share your revised sentences with a partner.

ordered	replied	laughed
bragged	cried	

1. "Why do you work so hard?" called Grasshopper. "Because I have work to do," _____ Ant.

2. "I'm gonna beat you. I'm gonna beat you," _____ Hare.

3. "You had better do what I say," _____ Ann. "Or Mom's going to be mad at you."

4. "Yow!" Anthony _____. "That really hurts!"

5. "That was the funniest play I've ever seen," _____ Joan.

Choose one sentence and draw a picture of it.
Share your picture with your partner.

Verb Match-Up

Read each column. Draw a line from the weak verb to its matching strong verb. Use a dictionary if needed.

Weak Verbs	**Strong Verbs**
give	describe
knock	create
tell	serve
fight	tackle
make	argue

Choose one strong verb. Use it in a sentence.

_____

_____

Assessment

Read the sentences. Choose a strong verb from the word bank and write it on the line provided.

slithered	joked	booed

1. "Toss him out," _____ the angry baseball crowd.

2. The snake _____ across the sand.

3. The coach _____ with his team before the final game.

Read the sentences. Replace the underlined weak verb with a strong verb.

1. The little boy yelled at his mother.

_____

_____

2. Can you say it again?

_____

_____

Overview   Nouns

Directions and Sample Answers for Activity Pages

Day 1	See "Provide a Real-World Example" below.
Day 2	Read the title and directions aloud. Invite students to read the nouns in both columns. Then ask students to draw lines matching each noun on the left side with its synonym on the right. Have students share responses with a partner. Finally, have students choose one noun from the right column and use it in a sentence. (Answers: plate—platter; couch—sofa; flower—bloom; box—chest; cloth—fabric; trash—litter)
Day 3	Read the title and directions aloud. Invite students to read the sentences. Ask students to choose nouns from the word bank that mean the same thing as the underlined words. Have students rewrite the sentences using the new nouns. (Answers: 1. visitors; 2. village; 3. battle; 4. den; 5. trinkets) Finally, ask students to choose a sentence and illustrate it.
Day 4	Read the title and directions aloud. Invite students to read the nouns in both columns. Then ask students to draw lines matching animals on the left side with their group names on the right side. Have students choose one animal and its group name and use it in a sentence. (Answers: ants—colony; fish—school; mules—pack; clams—bed; porcupines—prickle; chickens—brood; dolphins—pod)
Day 5	Read the directions aloud. Allow time for students to complete the tasks. (Answers: rock—stone, car—vehicle, mail—letter; 1. crop, 2. toddler, 3. lamp) Afterward, meet individually with students. Discuss their results. Use their responses to plan further instruction.

Provide a Real-World Example

◆ Hand out the Day 1 activity page. Write the word **noun** on the board. **Ask:** *What is a noun?* (Allow responses.) **Say:** *A noun is a word that names a person, place, thing, or idea. What are some person nouns?* (Allow responses.)

◆ **Say:** *We can use a noun to complete the first sentence.* (Model completing the first sentence with the noun **party**.) *Authors use nouns in their writing, but good authors want to use the noun that tells exactly what they are thinking. Let's think about how to use the best noun. Look at the sentence. The word **party** is a great noun. You have a lot of fun at a party, but the purpose for the party was to celebrate winning the game. Right? So I wonder if there is another noun that we could use in place of **party**. A noun that means something like **party**. A synonym for **party**.*

◆ Rewrite the sentence on the board using the term **victory celebration**.

◆ **Say:** *Now look at the sentence. I changed **party** to **celebration**. What do you think of when you hear the word **celebration**?* (Allow responses.)

◆ **Say:** *Party and celebration mean almost the same thing. In this case, celebration might be the better word to use. Remember, authors choose words that tell exactly what they feel. Think about what you really want to say and use the best words to say it.*

Nouns

person	place	thing	idea
sister, brother, mom, teacher	home, school, zoo, park	ball, shoe, dog, cat	love, peace

Nouns

Complete the chart.

Nouns

person	place	thing	idea

Complete the sentences.

My team won the game, so we had a _____.

My team won the game, so we had a _____.

Noun Match

Read the nouns in each column. Draw lines matching nouns on the left side of the page with their synonyms on the right side. Share your thinking with a partner. Use a dictionary to define words that you do not know.

Old Noun	**New Noun**
plate	bloom
couch	chest
flower	litter
box	platter
cloth	sofa
trash	fabric

Choose a noun from the right column and write a sentence using it.

_____

_____

Choose a Noun

Read the sentences. Choose nouns from the word bank that mean about the same thing as the underlined nouns. Rewrite the sentences using your new nouns. Share your sentences with a partner.

village	den	trinkets
visitors	battle	

"We don't get many <u>people</u> out here," the old lady said.

_____

The elves lived in a very small <u>town</u>.

_____

The <u>fight</u> between the two brothers went on for days.

_____

The bear's <u>home</u> was an old, burned-out tree.

_____

The children loved their little <u>toys</u>.

_____

Choose a sentence and draw a picture of it.

Animal Groups

A gaggle of geese? A covey of quail? Have you ever heard of these things? They are nouns that are used for animal groups. Read the list of animals on the left side of the page. Read the group names listed on the right. Draw lines matching animals to their group names. Use a dictionary if needed.

Animals	**Groups**
ants	pod
fish	brood
mules	colony
clams	pack
porcupines	bed
chickens	prickle
dolphins	school

Choose one animal and its group name. Use them in a sentence.

_____

_____

Assessment

**Read the nouns in each column. Draw lines matching nouns
on the left side to nouns on the right side.**

rock   letter

car   stone

mail   vehicle

**Read the sentences. Think about the underlined noun.
Choose a noun from the word bank that means about the same thing.
Rewrite the sentences using your new noun.**

| toddler | lamp | crop |

1. We gathered our fruit.

_____

2. The boy fell off the slide.

_____

3. Turn off the light.

_____

Overview   Idioms

Directions and Sample Answers for Activity Pages

Day 1	See "Provide a Real-World Example" below.
Day 2	Read the title and directions aloud. Invite students to read the sentences in both columns. Ask students to draw a line matching the sentence on the left with its corresponding sentence on the right. Have students share their results with a partner. (Answers: My doctor gave me a clean bill of health.—I'm in good health; Go fly a kite.—Go away and leave me alone; This game is driving me crazy.—This game is hard; That's the way the ball bounces.—Things don't always go your way.)
Day 3	Read the title and directions aloud. Invite students to read the sentences and tell what each sentence really means. Then have students draw a picture illustrating each sentence. Have students share thinking and illustrations with a partner. (Answers: 1. I told everyone what my mother was getting for her birthday. 2. It was raining really hard. 3. The math test was easy. 4. My dad likes things with sugar in them.)
Day 4	Read the title and directions aloud. Have students read the sentences. Then have students match the sentences to the idioms in the bank. Have students share their thinking with a partner. (Answer: 1. hold your tongue; 2. in hot water; 3. eyes in the back of her head; 4. apple of my eye) Finally, have students choose one idiom and use it in a sentence.
Day 5	Read the directions aloud. Allow time for students to complete the tasks. (Answers: 1. no one picked me as a partner; 2. I'm sad; 1. name is mud; 2. at the end of my rope; 3. bed of roses) Afterward, meet individually with students. Discuss their results. Use their responses to plan further instruction.

Provide a Real-World Example

◆ Hand out the Day 1 activity page. **Say:** *Authors want their writing to be interesting. They want to create pictures in the minds of their readers. Using idioms is one way to do this. An idiom is a way that people talk and write. What they say isn't really what they mean. You have to know the idiom to know what the meaning really is. You are going to learn idioms in this unit. Read the sentence on the board. I think I can rewrite that sentence using an idiom. I think it will be more interesting and create a picture in the reader's mind.*

◆ Revise the sentence with this example:
Jenny has a bee in her bonnet.

◆ **Say:** *Now read the sentence. Jenny doesn't really have a bee in her bonnet. The idiom "bee in her bonnet" means that Jenny is agitated or upset about something. Let's look at a few other idioms.*

◆ Repeat with the remaining sentences.

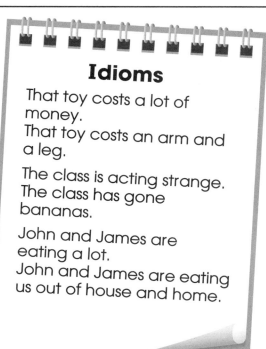

Idioms

That toy costs a lot of money.
That toy costs an arm and a leg.

The class is acting strange.
The class has gone bananas.

John and James are eating a lot.
John and James are eating us out of house and home.

Name _____

Idioms

Rewrite the sentences using idioms.

1. Jenny is upset.

_____

_____

2. That toy costs a lot of money.

_____

_____

3. The class is acting strange.

_____

_____

4. John and James are eating a lot.

_____

_____

Idiom Match

Read the sentences on the left side of the page. Then read the sentences on the right side of the page. Draw a line from the idiom sentence to its meaning. Share your results with a partner.

Idiom Sentences	**Plain Sentences**
My doctor gave me a clean bill of health.	Things don't always go your way.
Go fly a kite.	This game is hard.
This game is driving me crazy.	I'm in good health.
That's the way the ball bounces.	Go away and leave me alone.

Choose one of the idiom sentences and draw what it looks like to you. Ask a partner to choose which sentence you drew.

What Does It Really Mean?

Read the sentences and look at the underlined idiom phrase. Tell what each sentence really means. Then draw a picture describing each sentence. Share your thinking and drawings with a partner.

1. I spilled the beans. Now Mom knows what I'm getting her for her birthday.

_____

_____

2. We had to take an umbrella to the library. It was raining cats and dogs.

_____

_____

3. The math test was a piece of cake.

_____

_____

4. My dad has such a sweet tooth. If we leave cookies out, he eats them.

_____

_____

Writing with Idioms

**Read the sentences. What idiom could you use for each sentence?
Choose one from the idiom bank and write it on the line. Share your answers
with a partner.**

has eyes in the back of her head	hold your tongue	the apple of my eye	in hot water

1. Please don't say another word.

_____

2. We are in trouble.

_____

3. Mrs. Jones knows about everything that goes on in the classroom.

_____

4. My daughter is so special to me.

_____

Choose one idiom from the bank and use it in a sentence.

_____

Assessment

Read the sentences and look at the underlined idiom phrases.
Tell what each sentence really means.

1. I've been <u>left out in the cold</u> because no one wants to be my partner.

_____

_____

2. I'm <u>feeling blue</u> today.

_____

_____

Read the sentences. What idiom could you use for each sentence?
Choose one from the idiom bank and write it on the line.

bed of roses	at the end of my rope	name is mud

1. I'm in trouble.

_____

2. I don't know what to do.

_____

3. My life is so good right now.

_____

Overview Similes

Directions and Sample Answers for Activity Pages

Day 1	See "Provide a Real-World Example" below.
Day 2	Read the title and directions aloud. Invite students to read the sentences. Ask students to tell what is being compared. Then have them draw a picture illustrating the sentence. Have students share thinking and illustrations with a partner. (Answers: 1. gum compared to a rock; 2. person and hungry bear; 3. people and mice; 4. Paul and a turtle)
Day 3	Read the title and directions aloud. Invite students to read the sentences. Ask students to tell what is being compared. Then have them draw a picture illustrating the sentence. Have students share thinking and illustrations with a partner. (Answers: 1. brother and sister and fighting cats and dogs; 2. snow and blanket; 3. Sam and the wind; 4. Tammy and a bird)
Day 4	Read the title and directions aloud. Invite students to read the sentences in both columns. Ask students to draw a line matching the sentence on the left with its corresponding sentence on the right. Have students choose one sentence from the right side, tell what is being compared, and illustrate it. Have students share their thinking and illustrations with a partner. (Answers: These shoes are very comfortable—These shoes fit like a glove; Patty was cold—Patty was like an icicle; Bob can lift a lot—Bob is as strong as an ox; I eat a lot when I get home from school—I eat like a horse after school.)
Day 5	Read the directions aloud. Allow time for students to complete the task. (Answers: 1. a beach ball and a pancake—The sentence means the beach ball was out of air.; 2. a person and a bump on a log—The sentence is telling someone not to sit and do nothing.; 3. a person and a wink—The sentence is asking someone to clean the room quickly.; 4. my sister and a monkey—The sentence is saying that my sister talks a lot.) Afterward, meet individually with students. Discuss their results. Use their responses to plan further instruction.

Provide a Real-World Example

◆ Hand out the Day 1 activity page. **Say:** *Authors want their writing to be interesting. They want to create pictures in the minds of their readers. Using similes is one way to do this. A simile compares two things using the words* **like** *or* **as**. *Read the first sentence. I think I can rewrite that sentence using a simile. I think it will be more interesting and create a picture in the reader's mind.*

◆ Revise the sentence with the example below:
Jan swims like a fish.

◆ **Say:** *Now read the sentence. I compared Jan with a fish using the word* **like**. *I'm still saying that Jan is a good swimmer. But now, I'm saying it in a more colorful, interesting way. You can see Jan swimming in the pool just like a fish. You may even be able to draw a picture in your mind of Jan swimming but with a fish's body. That's kind of funny. Try drawing Jan as a swimming fish on your page. Let's look at another simile example.*

◆ Repeat with other examples.

Similes

A comparison using **like** or **as**.

Jan is a good swimmer.

Jan swims like a fish.

Jan is a busy person.

Jan is as busy as a bee.

Similes

Rewrite the sentences to include similes. Tell what is being compared. Then draw a picture showing what the sentence is telling you.

Jan is a good swimmer.

_____

What is being compared?

_____

Jan is a busy person.

_____

What is being compared?

_____

Picture This

Read the sentences using "as" similes. Under each sentence, tell what is being compared. Then draw a picture showing what the sentence is telling you. Share your thinking and drawings with a partner.

1. This gum is as hard as a rock.

What is being compared? _____

2. I woke up as hungry as a bear.

What is being compared? _____

3. When you walk down the hall, please be as quiet as mice.

What is being compared? _____

4. Paul never moves fast. He's as slow as a turtle.

What is being compared? _____

Picture This, Too

Read the sentences using "like" similes. Under each sentence, tell what is being compared. Then draw a picture showing what the sentence is telling you. Share your thinking and drawings with a partner.

1. My little brother and sister fight like cats and dogs.

What is being compared? _____

2. The snow was like a blanket. Our backyard was tucked in under it.

What is being compared? _____

3. I want Sam on my team. He can run like the wind.

What is being compared? _____

4. Tammy eats like a bird.

What is being compared? _____

Simile Match

Read the sentences in both columns. Sentences on the left do not have similes. Sentences on the right mean the same thing but have similes. Draw a line from the sentence on the left to its matching sentence on the right.

These shoes are very comfortable.	Patty was like an icicle.
Patty was cold.	I eat like a horse after school.
Bob can lift a lot.	These shoes fit like a glove.
I eat a lot when I get home from school.	Bob is as strong as an ox.

Choose one sentence from the right side. Tell what two things are being compared. Draw a picture showing what the sentence really means.

Assessment

**Read the sentences. Under each sentence, tell what is being compared.
Then tell what the sentence really means.**

1. My beach ball was as flat as a pancake.

What is being compared? _____

What does the sentence mean?

_____

_____

2. Please don't sit there like a bump on a log. Do something.

What is being compared? _____

What does the sentence mean?

_____

_____

3. Clean your room as quick as a wink and then we can go.

What is being compared? _____

What does the sentence mean?

_____

_____

4. My little sister chatters like a monkey.

What is being compared? _____

What does the sentence mean?

_____

_____

Overview   What Is a Sentence?

Directions and Sample Answers for Activity Pages

Day 1	See "Provide a Real-World Example" below.
Day 2	Read the title and directions aloud. Invite students to read each group of words. Ask students to decide if each group is a sentence fragment or a complete sentence. Have students label sentence fragments with an F and complete sentences with a C. Have students share responses with a partner. Finally, ask students to rewrite sentence fragments into complete sentences and share their new sentences with a partner. (Answers: C, F, F, C)
Day 3	Read the title and directions aloud. Invite students to read each sentence fragment and rewrite the fragments into complete sentences. Finally, ask students to choose one new sentence and illustrate it.
Day 4	Read the title and directions aloud. Invite students to read the sentence fragments in both columns. Ask students to make complete sentences by drawing lines from fragments in the left column to fragments in the right column. Finally, have students choose two sentences and illustrate them. Have students share their illustrations with a partner. (Answers: My little brother tore my homework. Our neighbor's cat caught a mouse. Do not mess with a bear's den. Can you bring cupcakes to school?)
Day 5	Read the directions aloud. Allow time for students to complete the tasks. (Answers: F, C, F, C; Afterward, meet individually with students to discuss results and plan further instruction.

Provide a Real-World Example

◆ Hand out the Day 1 activity page. **Ask:** *What do you see on this page? This is an eggshell* **fragment**. *The word* **fragment** *means not complete, or incomplete. A complete eggshell has all the pieces.* Write the word **fragment** under the picture of an eggshell fragment. Write the word **complete** under the picture of a complete eggshell.

◆ **Say:** *I think of an eggshell when I think of sentences. A sentence is a group of words that answers two questions— Who or what is the sentence about? and What happened in the sentence? We know that the who or what of a sentence is the noun—the person, place, thing, or idea. What happened in a sentence is the verb, or action.* Point out this information on the sidebar on the activity page.

◆ **Say:** *If the words don't answer both questions, then it is a sentence fragment. Look at the words* **an eggshell**. *Can I answer both questions? I can answer the first question. The words are about an eggshell, a thing. Can I answer the second question? What happened to the eggshell? No, the words do not answer that question. Nothing happened to the eggshell. These words make a sentence fragment.*

◆ **Say:** *I can add a verb, or action, to the words and make a sentence. An eggshell* **breaks**.

◆ **Ask:** *Now can I answer the second question? Yes. What happens to the eggshell?* (Allow responses.) *Yes. The eggshell breaks.* **Break** *is a verb, or action word. I can even add more to this sentence to make it more interesting. Notice that I used a capital letter and a period in my sentence.*

◆ Repeat by having students form sentences with other fragments.

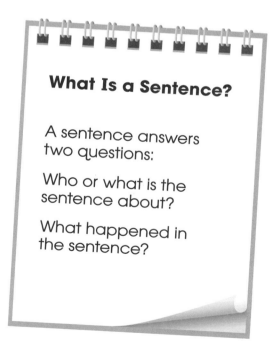

What Is a Sentence?

A sentence answers two questions:

Who or what is the sentence about?

What happened in the sentence?

What Is a Sentence?

Rewrite the words to make sentences.

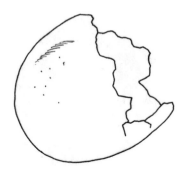   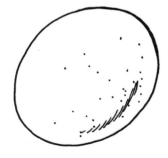

_____   _____

an eggshell

_____

_____

sits on the front porch

_____

_____

my ice cream cone

_____

_____

slipped

_____

_____

Fragment or Not?

Read each group of words. Put an F by the words that are sentence fragments. Put a C by the words that are complete sentences. (Clue: There are two sentence fragments and two complete sentences.) Share your answers with a partner.

☐ I spilled water on my book.

☐ Hot outside.

☐ The ball.

☐ The bird flew from the cage.

Rewrite the sentence fragments into complete sentences. Share your sentences with a partner.

_____

_____

_____

_____

Rewrite Fragments

Rewrite the sentence fragments into complete sentences. Remember to add details, capital letters, and periods.

1. some people

_____

_____

2. runs in the race

_____

_____

3. found a home

_____

_____

4. the spider

_____

_____

Choose one sentence. Draw a picture of the sentence.

Fragment Match-Up

Read the sentence fragments in both columns. Make complete sentences by drawing lines from the fragments in the left column to fragments in the right column. Share your answers with a partner.

Who or What	**What Happened?**
My little brother	a bear's den.
Our neighbor's cat	tore my homework.
Do not mess with	cupcakes to school?
Can you bring	caught a mouse.

Choose two sentences. Draw a picture for each sentence. Share your drawings with a partner. Can your partner guess which sentences you drew?

Assessment

Read each group of words. Put an F by the words that are sentence fragments. Put a C by the words that are complete sentences.

☐	Made a cake.
☐	John painted birdhouses.
☐	Our football team.
☐	The glass lamp broke.

Read each sentence fragment. Rewrite the words into complete sentences. Remember to add details, capital letters, and periods.

1. the grass

_____

_____

2. jumped out of the box

_____

_____

Overview Varying Sentence Structure

Directions and Sample Answers for Activity Pages

Day 1	See "Provide a Real-World Example" below.
Day 2	Read the title and directions aloud. Invite students to read each sentence and question. Tell them that the answer to each question adds detail to each sentence. Have students rewrite the sentences and include the answers to the questions. Finally, have students choose one sentence and illustrate it.
Day 3	Read the title and directions aloud. Invite students to read the sentences in the sentence bank. Then ask students to read the sentence pairs. Have students match sentence pairs to the correct sentence in the bank and write it on the line. Finally, ask students to illustrate each answer. (The cat jumped out of the tree and ran to the backyard; My brother John goes to college; It was hot when the parade started at ten o'clock; The tall glass is green.)
Day 4	Read the title and directions aloud. Invite students to read the sentence pairs. Ask students to combine pairs into one sentence. Have students choose one combined sentence and illustrate it. If students struggle, have them review sentences from Day 3. (Possible answers: 1. The boy laughed and fell off the bunk bed. 2. The crooked tree is dead. 3. Dad mowed the grass on Sunday. 4. The car was in the garage because it had a flat tire.)
Day 5	Read the directions aloud. Allow time for students to complete the task. (Possible answers: 1. Michael fell in the dirt. 2. The butterfly flew away because of the rain.) Then have students complete the second task. (Possible answers: 1. My aunt loves cookies and hamburgers. 2. The boys found pretty shells on the beach.) Afterward, meet individually with students. Discuss their results. Use their responses to plan further instruction.

Provide a Real-World Example

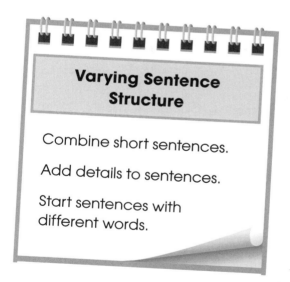

Varying Sentence Structure

Combine short sentences.

Add details to sentences.

Start sentences with different words.

◆ Hand out the Day 1 activity page. Have a student read the paragraph. **Ask:** *What is this paragraph about?* (Allow responses.) *What does this paragraph tell us about snow?*

◆ **Say:** *This paragraph gives good information about snow, but it doesn't sound very interesting. What do you notice about the sentences?* (Allow responses.)

◆ **Say:** *Yes. The sentences look alike, or similar. One way that authors make their writing interesting is to change the way their sentences look and sound. Each of these sentences starts with "it is" or "it does." I bet I can make this paragraph more interesting. I can do that three different ways. I can start sentences with different words. I can combine short sentences, and I can add details.*

◆ **Say:** *Watch as I rewrite this paragraph. Snow is very interesting. It is very cold when it hits your face, but then it melts because snow is just ice. It does not snow everywhere. Snow falls all the time in the north, but not so much in the south. This is because it is colder in the north than in the south. Wherever you live, snow is fun.*

◆ **Say:** *Now look at my paragraph. It's definitely longer, but it also sounds better and says more about snow.* Have a student read the revised paragraph. Then have students practice writing their own revised paragraphs on their handout.

Varying Sentence Structure

Rewrite the following paragraph.

Snow is very interesting. It is cold. It is wet. It does not snow everywhere. It is fun.

_____

_____

_____

_____

_____

_____

_____

Add Detail

Read each sentence. Read the question after each sentence. Add details to the sentence to answer the question. Rewrite the sentence on the lines.

1. My cat slept. (Where did the cat sleep?)

_____

_____

2. John ran. (When did John run?)

_____

_____

3. Amy was mad. (Why was Amy mad?)

_____

_____

4. It was raining outside. (What did you do because it was raining outside?)

_____

_____

Choose one sentence that you have changed. Draw a picture of the sentence.

Sentence Match-Up

Read the sentence pairs. Match the sentence pairs with the correct combined sentence from the sentence bank and write it on the lines.

| My brother John goes to college. | The cat jumped out of the tree and ran to the backyard. | The tall glass is green. | It was hot when the parade started at ten o'clock. |

The cat jumped out of the tree.
The cat ran to the backyard.

_____
_____
_____

John is my brother.
He goes to college.

_____
_____
_____

The parade started at ten o'clock.
It was very hot when the
parade started.

_____
_____
_____

The glass is tall. The glass is green.

_____
_____

Choose one combined sentence and draw a picture of it.

Unit 20 • Everyday Writing Intervention Activities Grade 3 • © 2011 Newmark Learning, LLC

Combining Sentences

Read the sentences. Combine them into one sentence.

1. The boy laughed. The boy fell off the bunk bed.

_____

_____

2. The tree is crooked. The tree is dead.

_____

_____

3. Dad mowed the grass. It was Sunday.

_____

_____

4. The car was in the garage. The car had a flat tire.

_____

_____

Choose one combined sentence and draw a picture of it.

Assessment

Read each sentence. Read the question after each sentence. Add details to the sentence that answers the question. Rewrite the sentence on the lines.

1. Michael fell. (Where did Michael fall?)

_____

_____

2. The butterfly flew away. (Why did the butterfly fly away?)

_____

_____

**Read the sentences. Combine them into one sentence.
Share your sentence with a partner.**

1. My aunt loves cookies.
   My aunt loves hamburgers.

_____

_____

2. The boys found shells on the beach.
   The shells were pretty.

_____

_____